LEGENDS FROM MEXICO & CENTRAL AMERICA

A QUETZALCÓATL
TALE OF CHOCOLATE

Retold by Marilyn Parke and Sharon Panik
Illustrations by Lynn Castle

Consultants to the Series
R. Robert and Maria Elena Robbins

Fearon Teacher Aids
A Paramount Communications Company

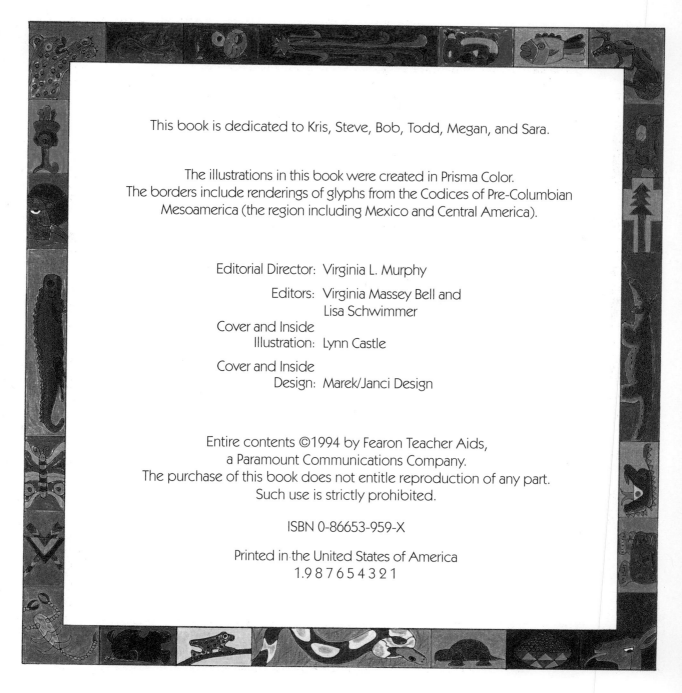

This book is dedicated to Kris, Steve, Bob, Todd, Megan, and Sara.

The illustrations in this book were created in Prisma Color.
The borders include renderings of glyphs from the Codices of Pre-Columbian
Mesoamerica (the region including Mexico and Central America).

Editorial Director: Virginia L. Murphy

Editors: Virginia Massey Bell and
Lisa Schwimmer

Cover and Inside
Illustration: Lynn Castle

Cover and Inside
Design: Marek/Janci Design

ISBN 0-86653-959-X

Printed in the United States of America
1 9 8 7 6 5 4 3 2 1

Throughout the ages, stories of Quetzalcóatl have been part of the Maya, Aztec, and Mexican cultures. Over the years, these stories were subject to different interpretations, first by the native people themselves, and later by the Spanish missionary friars who established the first written record of these legends.

Historians, anthropologists, and ethnographers continue to refine these earlier interpretations. The authors' intent in this series is to revive the spirit of the oral tradition in a format available to children.

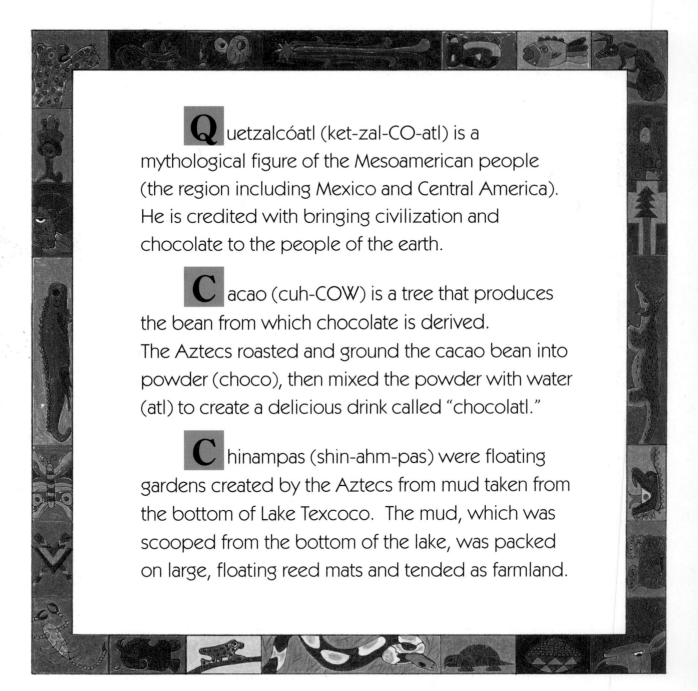

Quetzalcóatl (ket-zal-CO-atl) is a mythological figure of the Mesoamerican people (the region including Mexico and Central America). He is credited with bringing civilization and chocolate to the people of the earth.

Cacao (cuh-COW) is a tree that produces the bean from which chocolate is derived. The Aztecs roasted and ground the cacao bean into powder (choco), then mixed the powder with water (atl) to create a delicious drink called "chocolatl."

Chinampas (shin-ahm-pas) were floating gardens created by the Aztecs from mud taken from the bottom of Lake Texcoco. The mud, which was scooped from the bottom of the lake, was packed on large, floating reed mats and tended as farmland.

Quetzalcóatl, the priest, gathered the children around the fire. He told them a story of the old, old days of his ancestor, Quetzalcóatl, the god. He told them first that Quetzalcóatl was a great civilizer, the bringer of corn, a competitor of Tlaloc's in the first ball game, and the provider of chocolate to the people of the earth. This is the story that he told.

Dicen que (they say that) long ago humans were told to leave the jungle garden of the gods. The people were sent to live near jungles of their own on earth, where most of the time they were happy.

Two Wind Deer was a farmer's son who lived with his family in a jungle village. He and his family belonged to the Shining Jaguar clan. Two Wind Deer was proud to be a member of this brave and honorable group. The Shining Jaguar clan were hard workers, skilled craftsmen, brave warriors, kind, and cheerful.

9

Two Wind Deer and the people of the village had plenty of food to eat, both from the lakes and from the streams — they ate turtles, manatees, crocodiles, and fish.

12

Two Wind Deer and the hunters from his village used bows and arrows, snares, and atlatls to hunt for deer, turkeys, armadillos, and other animals.

Sometimes the hunters used blowguns with pellets to shoot ducks, pigeons, and quail as they flew through the air.

16

In their chinampas, village farmers grew corn, beans, squash, melons, sweet potatoes, fruits, and other vegetables. The villagers always had plenty to eat.

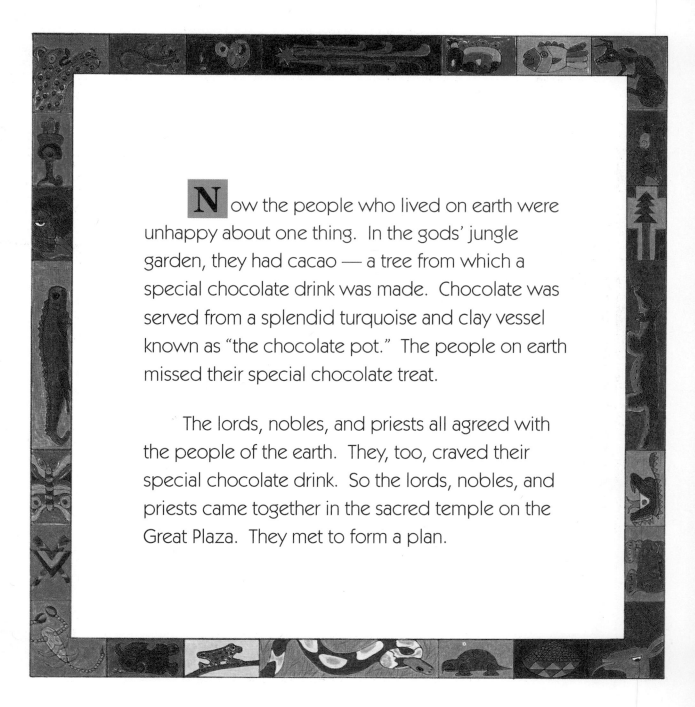

Now the people who lived on earth were unhappy about one thing. In the gods' jungle garden, they had cacao — a tree from which a special chocolate drink was made. Chocolate was served from a splendid turquoise and clay vessel known as "the chocolate pot." The people on earth missed their special chocolate treat.

The lords, nobles, and priests all agreed with the people of the earth. They, too, craved their special chocolate drink. So the lords, nobles, and priests came together in the sacred temple on the Great Plaza. They met to form a plan.

21

At the same time the priests, lords, and nobles were meeting in the temple, Two Wind Deer and his pet monkey were playing ball nearby. Two Wind Deer gave a mighty toss and accidentally threw his rubber ball across the plaza and into the sacred temple.

Monkey scampered after the ball while Two Wind Deer quickly followed. Once inside the forbidden place, Two Wind Deer found the lords, nobles, and priests in a serious conversation.

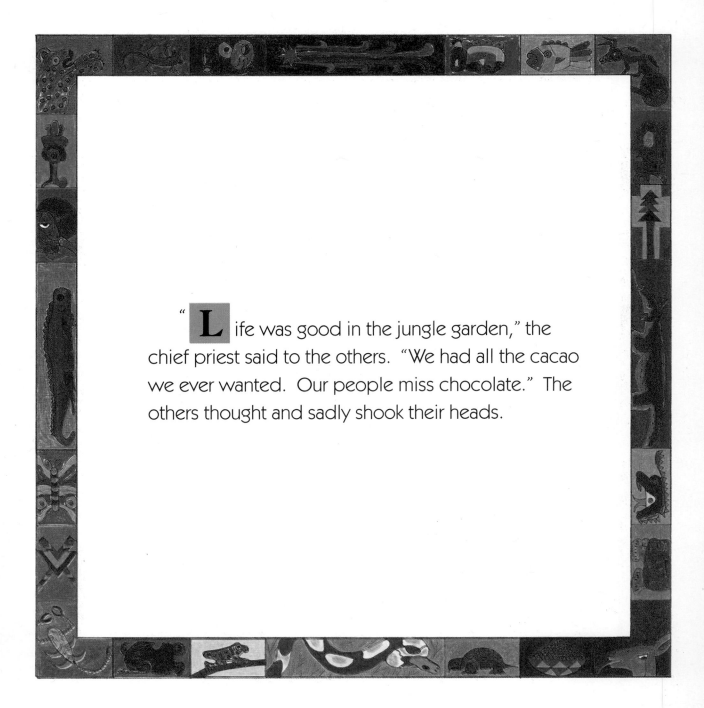

"Life was good in the jungle garden," the chief priest said to the others. "We had all the cacao we ever wanted. Our people miss chocolate." The others thought and sadly shook their heads.

27

From the corner where he was hiding, Two Wind Deer said without thinking, "Quetzalcóatl might help us. When we lived in the jungle garden, my family sat under the cacao tree where Quetzalcóatl let us drink chocolate from his golden goblet. Sometimes we mixed the chocolate drink with maize flour. I liked the drink best with honey, but my father liked his chocolate with chili."

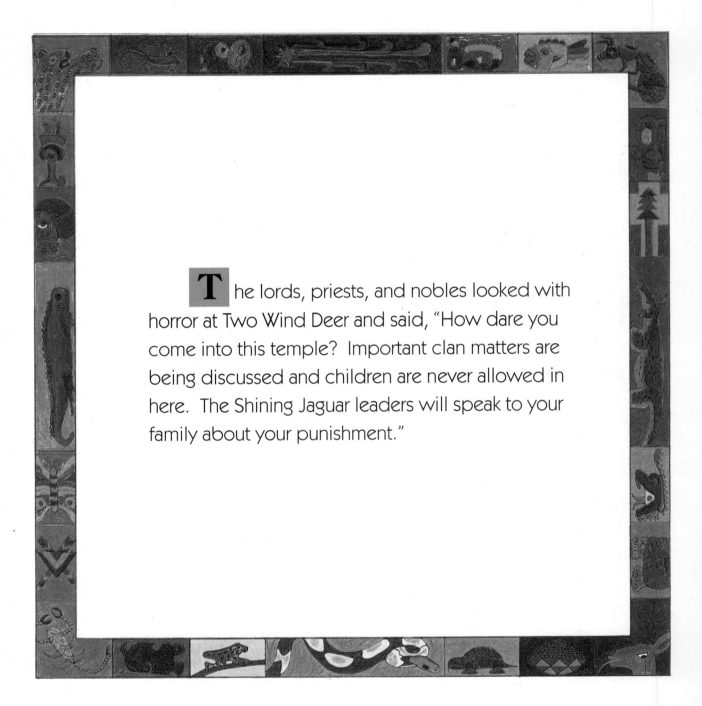

The lords, priests, and nobles looked with horror at Two Wind Deer and said, "How dare you come into this temple? Important clan matters are being discussed and children are never allowed in here. The Shining Jaguar leaders will speak to your family about your punishment."

31

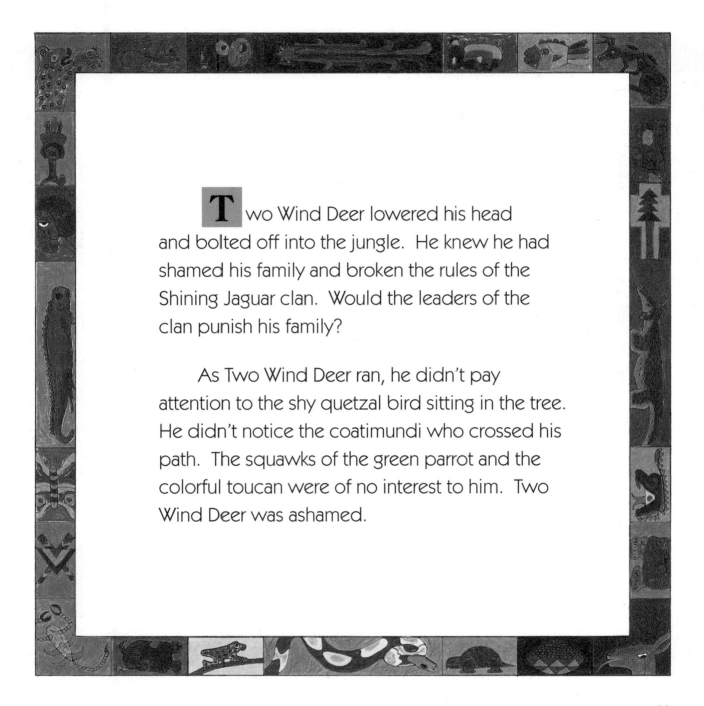

Two Wind Deer lowered his head and bolted off into the jungle. He knew he had shamed his family and broken the rules of the Shining Jaguar clan. Would the leaders of the clan punish his family?

As Two Wind Deer ran, he didn't pay attention to the shy quetzal bird sitting in the tree. He didn't notice the coatimundi who crossed his path. The squawks of the green parrot and the colorful toucan were of no interest to him. Two Wind Deer was ashamed.

Two Wind Deer wandered farther and farther into the dark jungle where he was frightened by the strange night sounds. Two Wind Deer longed to go home, even though he knew he would have to face his punishment . . . but where was home? Two Wind Deer was lost.

36

Two Wind Deer began to cry. Suddenly, he felt a warm and gentle hand — the hand of his pet monkey.

Two Wind Deer turned to Monkey and started to scold him. "Monkey, this is all your fault. I'll never find home, and even if I do, I will live forever in disgrace."

40

Monkey hugged Two Wind Deer and gently took him by the hand. He led him to a special place.

Two Wind Deer and Monkey entered a magical grove where the stars were shining brightly and the moon illuminated the many jungle trees. Monkey pulled Two Wind Deer to the center of the forest where there stood the largest, most beautiful cacao tree that Two Wind Deer had ever seen.

Monkey said in a soft and comforting voice, "Two Wind Deer, here is the cacao pod that you need. There are chocolate beans inside. Take this treasure to your village. The elders of the clan will not be angry with you anymore. You will no longer bring shame to your family."

Two Wind Deer smiled at Monkey.
Then, before his very eyes, he watched as Monkey
transformed into the mighty Quetzalcóatl.

45

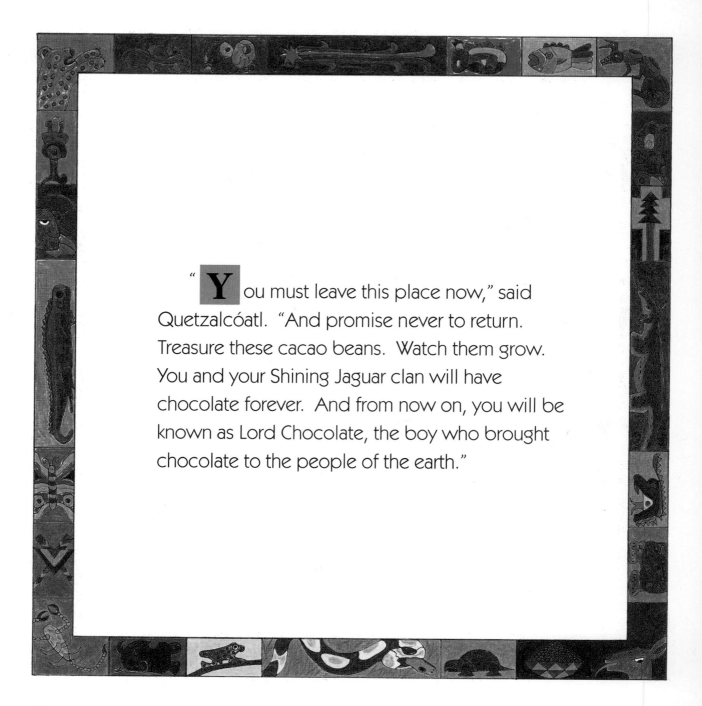

"**Y**ou must leave this place now," said Quetzalcóatl. "And promise never to return. Treasure these cacao beans. Watch them grow. You and your Shining Jaguar clan will have chocolate forever. And from now on, you will be known as Lord Chocolate, the boy who brought chocolate to the people of the earth."

Consultants

E.W. Adams	Ph.D., Archaeologist, University of Texas, San Antonio, Texas
Richard Ammon	Author, Middletown, Pennsylvania
Dr. Rosita Arvigo	Director, IX Chel Tropical Research Centre, San Ignacio, Cayo, Belize
Frances Berdan	Ph.D., Chair and Professor, Department of Anthropology, California State University, San Bernardino, California
Inga Calvin	Epigrapher, Denver Art Museum, Denver, Colorado
Chocolate Manufacturers Association of America	McLean, Virginia
Jane Stevenson Day	Ph.D., Chief Curator of Archaeology, Denver Museum of Natural History, Denver, Colorado
Ghiradelli Chocolate Company	San Leandro, California
Hershey Food	Hershey, Pennsylvania
Carlos Lopez	Mexico City, Mexico
Mary Lou Lovett	Art Instructor, Poudre School District, Fort Collins, Colorado
Emma Martinez	Educator, Chapter 1, Poudre School District, Fort Collins, Colorado
Lynette Marvin	Educator, Chapter 1, Poudre School District, Fort Collins, Colorado
Gordon McEwan	Ph.D., Curator, Art of the Americas, Denver Art Museum, Denver, Colorado
MaryJean Nelson	Ph.D., Art Historian, Coronado, California
Robert V. Parke	Ph.D., Former Chairman, Department of Botany, Colorado State University, Fort Collins, Colorado
Perry Ragouzis	Ph.D., Former Chairman, Department of Art, Colorado State University, Fort Collins, Colorado
Maria Elena Robbins	Translator and Educator, Austin, Texas
R. Robert Robbins	Ph.D., Archaeo-Astronomer, University of Texas, Austin, Texas
George Stewart	Ph.D., Archaeologist, National Geographic Magazine, Washington, D.C.
John A. West	Ph.D., Phycologist, University of California, Berkeley, California
Yvonne Wittreich	Ed.D., Chapter 1 Coordinator, Poudre School District, Fort Collins, Colorado